Published by Sweet Cherry Publishing Limited
Unit 36, Vulcan House,
Vulcan Road,
Leicester, LE5 3EF
United Kingdom

First published in the US in 2022
2022 edition

2 4 6 8 10 9 7 5 3 1

ISBN: 978-1-80263-051-0

Soccer Rising Stars: Bukayo Saka

Cover design and illustrations
by Sophie Jones

Lexile® code numerical measure L = Lexile® 950L

www.sweetcherrypublishing.com

Printed and bound in Turkey

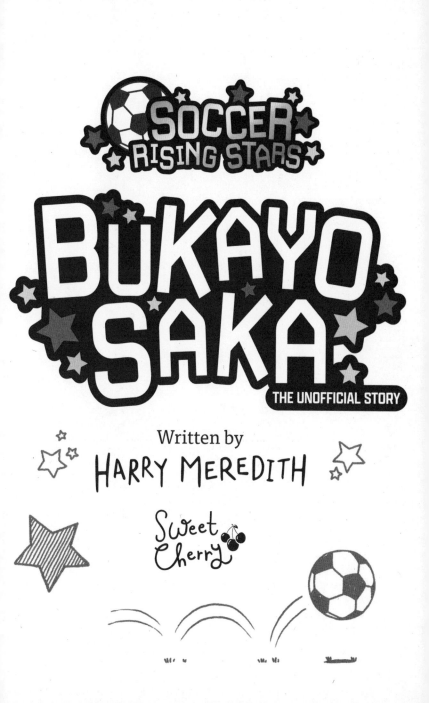

SOCCER RISING STARS

BUKAYO SAKA

THE UNOFFICIAL STORY

Written by
HARRY MEREDITH

Sweet Cherry

CONTENTS

SAKA THE SAVIOR

Arsenal FC have been a top side throughout most of the club's history. "The Gunners" have competed at the highest level, with a trophy cabinet to be proud of. But the club has not had recent success, having last won the Premier League trophy in the

2003/2004 season. Since then, their trophy cabinet has been collecting more dust than silverware, leaving Arsenal's fans dreaming of a return to soccer glory.

Arsenal's 2021/2022 Premier League season could hardly have got off to a worse start. The club had three back-to-back defeats at the hands of Brentford, Chelsea and Manchester City. The club bounced back with two 1-0 victories against

Norwich and Burnley, but their next was a match that they couldn't afford to lose.

Arsenal were playing their fierce rivals Tottenham Hotspur.

Thousands of fans had made their way to Arsenal's home stadium, the Emirates, to watch a mighty clash between the two capital city teams. This was a London derby with much more at stake than three points: there was pride and local bragging rights too.

The starting lineups for both sides were standing in the tunnel. There were no handshakes, smiles or friendly greetings between the two teams. Arsenal's captain, Pierre-Emerick Aubameyang, led his team

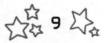

out of the tunnel. The players were greeted by deafening roars from the home fans. Behind Aubameyang was a fairly young team. Arsenal's performances over the past few years had not been the best. But this meant that a number of promising young players were given the opportunity to play first-team soccer in the hope of turning things around.

One of those young players, Bukayo Saka, had done far more than earn his place in the first team. In a period of gloom, Bukayo had been a shining light for his club—always playing

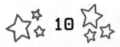

without fear and performing when his team needed him most. And on this day, against his club's fierce rivals, Bukayo needed to perform once more.

The Arsenal side, energized by the cheering crowd, started the match fiercely. They pressed their opponents and pounced onto every loose ball. In the 12th minute, new summer signing Martin Ødegaard, rushed into the opposition's half. He looked to his right and saw Bukayo sprinting forward. Ødegaard sent the ball to Bukayo, who was met by a number of

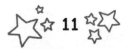

Tottenham defenders on the corner of their box. Unfazed by them, Bukayo swept his way into the box, confused the defense with a step over, and darted to the byline. Then he coolly slotted the ball into the path of his teammate Emile Smith Rowe, who fired it into the net. *Goal!*

The Arsenal fans in the stadium erupted. Taking the lead in any game made the fans feel good, but to do it against their local rivals felt ten times better.

Aware that they had their opponents on the back foot, Arsenal

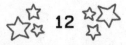

refused to let up. In the 27th minute, Aubameyang delicately flicked the ball into space from the halfway line. Smith Rowe sprinted forward with the ball. The chasing defenders couldn't get near him.

Bukayo ran faster than any of his teammates and was the first to reach the penalty area. By doing this, Bukayo had drawn the Tottenham defense toward him, and a gap had appeared at the edge of the box.

Aubameyang ran into the gap and Smith Rowe passed the ball to him.

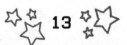

Arsenal's captain swung his left foot at the ball, and Tottenham's goalkeeper Hugo Lloris could do nothing as it bounced past him and into the net. *Goal!* Arsenal were dominating the match.

Then Harry Kane got possession of the ball and started off a Tottenham attack. He tried to confuse the Arsenal defenders with a ball roll but instead confused himself! The striker fell over his own feet, and Arsenal launched a counterattack.

Smith Rowe played the ball over to the right where Bukayo was in space.

Bukayo ran at the few remaining defenders in Tottenham's half and made his way to the penalty box. He tried to pass the ball to a teammate, but it was blocked by a defender. Fortunately, the ball bounced back to Bukayo's feet, and he brought it under his control once more. He wasn't going to let this second chance pass him by.

Bukayo fired the ball with his weaker right foot, and as it hit the  net, the home fans cheered in delight. It was 3-0! Bukayo ran to the corner

to celebrate with the fans. He slid on his knees and spread his arms out like a soaring eagle. The day was Arsenal's.

Bukayo helped lead his team to a 3-1 victory. The young star had been studying for his exams only a few years ago, and now he was the reason that thousands of Gunners fans were heading home from the station with smiles on their faces.

At just the age of 19, Bukayo had helped to dismantle his club's fiercest rivals. If he was capable of putting on performances like this at such a young age, there was no

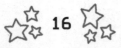

telling just how much this young talent could achieve. In a time where Arsenal needed a hero, one had been developing right under their nose at the academy.

2
A BROKEN FENCE

Bukayo Saka was born on the 5th of September 2001, and the London Borough of Ealing was his home. He was born to two Nigerian parents who had emigrated to England in search of work. Bukayo's parents strived to do their best for their children while also

sending some money back to family
in Nigeria too. Bukayo was a shining
light for them from the day he was
born. His parents named him Bukayo,
meaning "adds to happiness"—a
name that comes from the southern
Nigerian language of the Yoruba.
Their hope was that no matter where
Bukayo was in the world, he would
bring a smile to the faces of everyone
he met.

As part of a loving family, Bukayo
grew up gentle, hard working and
honest. He studied as hard as he could
in the classroom, but when the final

bell rang at the end of the school day, he chased his true passion.

Bukayo played soccer whenever he got the chance, whether he was testing his skills against his friends on the local park, or working on his close control in his back garden.

One day after school, Bukayo went straight to his garden and flicked a ball into the air. He wanted to make it all the way to fifty keepy uppies this time. He easily made it to ten before testing himself with his weaker right foot. He passed twenty and started to switch between both feet. He reached thirty and began to use his knees too. Then, as he reached forty, he challenged himself to use his head as well.

... Forty-five, forty-six, forty-seven, forty-eight ...

The headers forced him backward, and Bukayo lost control. On the forty-ninth keepy uppy, the ball bounced off his head at an odd angle. Bukayo almost cried out in frustration at the thought of so narrowly missing his target. But as the ball fell to the ground, Bukayo shifted forward and stuck out his leg. The ball made contact. He'd made it to fifty! But the

ball had hit the garden fence. The old, damp wooden planks splintered under the force of it. Pieces of broken fence toppled over onto his next-door neighbor's flower bed.

Bukayo held his hands behind his head and closed his eyes, grimacing. *Uh-oh ...*

"Bukayo!" shouted his father, bursting out of the back door at the sound of the fence breaking. "What on earth have you done?"

Bukayo was made to knock on the neighbor's door and apologize for the damage. Although he got his ball

back, there was to be no more playing soccer in the garden. But Bukayo's father knew that his son was talented. He wanted to nurture his son's love of soccer, and he understood that Bukayo needed a better environment to practice in. It was time for Bukayo to join a team.

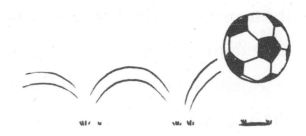

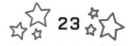

3
OUT OF THE HOUSE

On a cold Sunday morning, with a light mist covering Perivale Park, Bukayo and his father approached the manager of a local soccer team: Greenford Celtic FC.

"Are you here for the trials?" asked the manager.

"We are," said Bukayo's father. "This is my son Bukayo."

"Nice to meet you, son," said the manager. "How old are you?"

"I'm 6," said Bukayo, clutching his cleat bag to his chest.

"Well, that's our youngest age group," said the manager. "Always good to get started as soon as possible. You never know, maybe we can make a professional soccer player out of you!"

Bukayo ran over to a group of kids wearing brightly colored bibs. Before he knew it, he was on trial. The first exercises tested the players' fitness.

The kids had to run from one side of the field to the other, and Bukayo's energy was clear from the start. Before long, he was well ahead of the others. It wasn't just his speed that was on show, but his incredible stamina and competitiveness.

The coaches noted Bukayo's fitness, but they were yet to see him actually kick a ball. It was great that Bukayo was quick, but that wouldn't

count for much if he had two left feet.

Bukayo blew the rest of the competition away

during passing drills. Sometimes it took three of the other children to take the ball from him. It was clear that Bukayo was a natural talent. Before the trials had even finished, one of the coaches had made their way over to Bukayo's father.

"Your son has got something special," said the coach. "No doubt about it, he's A-team material. Welcome to the club."

"Great! I'll start bringing him over for regular practice," said Bukayo's father with a huge grin. Bursting with pride, he glanced at his son and gave

him a thumbs up. Bukayo's face lit up before he gave a thumbs up in return.

Back garden kickabouts became a thing of the past. They'd been replaced with regular training at the park and weekly matches against local teams in the same age group.

As Bukayo had shown during the trials, he was a natural talent. His competitive spirit and enthusiasm for the game made him one to watch. And the soccer scouts certainly did watch him. By the age of 7, Bukayo was already a hot prospect. His performances for Greenford Celtic

had put him on the radar of scouts at several soccer academies.

Bukayo received offers from a number of professional clubs, but none of those teams were the right fit. He spent some time training with Watford FC. However, it was another team from the capital that was able to entice Bukayo into a trial run at their academy. This club played in red rather than yellow.

The team that had come knocking on Bukayo's door was none other than Arsenal FC.

4

AN EXCELLENT STUDENT

When Bukayo arrived for his first day at the academy, he couldn't stop smiling. He would not be able to sign a full academy contract until he turned 9, but this trial period was

an enormous step. He didn't want to mess it up.

The scout who had found him, alongside the youth academy coordinator, met Bukayo at the entrance to the facilities.

"Welcome, Bukayo," said the coordinator with a smile. "Let's get you settled in."

As they walked down a corridor, Bukayo looked over the framed photographs on the walls. He stopped

by a picture of Jack Wilshere—a player who Arsenal had developed

at the academy, and who had recently made a breakthrough into the first team.

"That's a reminder for all of us," said the scout. "A reminder that what we do here on these training fieldes can have a real impact on our lives."

Bukayo followed them around the building. His jaw dropped at every turn as he took in the impressive facilities. There were gyms, locker rooms, plush offices and training areas galore.

However, it wasn't until they walked outside, with the cold air sending goosebumps across his body, that Bukayo started to feel at home.

The training fieldes were filled with tens if not hundreds of players. There were several age groups, including both children and teenagers. But Bukayo and his tour guides did not stay out in the cold with them for long, because Bukayo's teammates were in a classroom rather than on one of the fieldes.

The club wanted to educate their players for a life in soccer, but also

for one outside of it. Although their goal was for every single academy player to progress to the first team, that was not always possibile. It was important to prepare players for either outcome, just in case.

The coordinator knocked on the classroom door and entered, motioning for Bukayo to follow him.

"Ah, you must be Bukayo," said the teacher of the class. "Come in and take a seat. I'm just about to start a geography lesson."

All of the players' eyes zoned in on

the new boy. Bukayo didn't usually get nervous, but he couldn't help it as all of their attention focused on him.

"There's a seat next to me, Sir," said one of the players.

Bukayo walked over to the boy who had spoken, and pulled out the chair to sit down at the desk.

"Here's a notebook and pen," said the teacher, before returning to the front of the classroom. "Before we start, can we all say hello to Bukayo?"

"Hello! Hi! Morning!" shouted the other kids.

The warm welcome put Bukayo's

nerves at ease, and he grinned.

"I suppose we had better get started then," said the teacher. "Let's start with some quick-fire capital cities. Let's start with an easy one ... France!"

Bukayo's hand was the first to shoot up. The teacher picked him.

"Paris," said Bukayo.

"Excellent," said the teacher. "That was lighting quick. How about something trickier ... Ukraine?"

Bukayo knew the answer straight away, and once more his arm was up before anyone else's. The teacher picked him again.

"It's Kyiv," said Bukayo.

"Correct again. That's impressive," said the teacher. "I can tell you now, Bukayo, you're going to do very well here if you keep this up!"

5
SOCCER WITH FATHER

While Bukayo was learning his trade
at Arsenal, they quickly became
his favorite club. Bukayo's father,
however, was an avid Newcastle
United supporter. This was because
he was a massive fan of Alan
Shearer—the striker who holds the

record for the most Premier League goals scored at a whopping 260.

When Bukayo was 8 years old, his father took him to watch Newcastle play. Although Bukayo played for an academy, he had not been able to attend many professional soccer matches. Newcastle wasn't the team he supported, but Bukayo was very excited to go and watch a live soccer match. It was a chance to take a break from the academy, and to enjoy being part of a vibrant crowd in a real stadium.

The fixture was Manchester United vs Newcastle United at Old Trafford.

Bukayo and his father traveled all the way up to Manchester by train, laughing and joking, excited for the game. When they finally arrived, Bukayo's father proudly walked through the Manchester streets wearing his black-and-white Newcastle home gear. He didn't care that the majority of fans were supporting Manchester United or that he received some odd looks as they walked. Newcastle was his team, and Bukayo's father was proud to support them. Although his icon Alan Shearer had retired a couple of years earlier, he still followed The Magpies every soccer season.

Bukayo followed his father closely as they made their way through the thousands of supporters outside the stadium. The atmosphere felt like a carnival rather than a cold day up north. The sounds of excited voices and chants filled the streets. There were fathers and sons, mothers and daughters—entire families coming together for a special day out to watch the soccer.

As they walked through the crowds, the matchday scents drifted through

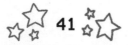

the air. There was the smell of burger vans with frying onions, hot drinks and even the occasional whiff of horse dung as local police officers paraded the streets on horses.

"Get your scarves and hats!" shouted a vendor. Bukayo and his father were getting close to the stadium, and they passed a merchandise stall. "We've got badges too. Get your matchday badges. Get them before they're gone."

Bukayo looked at the stall. There were scarves, woolen hats and hundreds of badges on a display. Noticing that Bukayo had stopped, his father hurried him along before the vendor could try to sell them anything.

They lined up to enter Old Trafford outside of the turnstiles. The turnstile clicked as they showed their tickets and entered the ground. They walked up endless flights of stairs, before finally making their way to their seats.

Bukayo looked in amazement at the players warming up on the field. There were stars for both teams only a few meters away. He was seeing professional soccer players in the flesh rather than on a television screen.

After loosening up, the players

applauded the fans and ran into the changing rooms. The surround speakers in the stadium were playing dramatic music to build up the tension for a clash between two historic soccer clubs.

A few minutes passed by, and then the referees led the players out from the tunnel to thunderous cheers. The game was about to start.

"It's exciting isn't it?" said Bukayo's father, trying his best to shout over the claps and cheers of the fans around him.

"It really is!" said Bukayo, eyes fixed

in wonder on the full stands.

"This could be you for Arsenal one day," said his father.

"I hope so," said Bukayo. "I'm going to give it my absolute best."

6
HALE END ACADEMY

When Bukayo wasn't in the classroom, he was learning his trade on the soccer fieldes at the academy. Bukayo had impressed everyone at the club, and at the age of 9 he signed his first academy contract. However, this was only the beginning of Bukayo's career

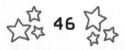

at Arsenal's academy. He would have to put in a lot more work to make it all the way.

It was clear to everyone that Bukayo had incredible natural ability. He had the pace, the strength and a left foot to be feared. But within an academy setup, the competition is so fierce that almost every player has natural ability. It is how a player trains and maximizes their potential through learning that makes the difference.

One aspect of Bukayo's game that vastly improved at the academy was his communication on the field.

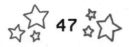

In such a competitive environment, this helped Bukayo to stand out in the crowd.

Bukayo continued to exceed expectations. As a reward for his hard work, he progressed through the age groups at Arsenal. Every new year at the academy, Bukayo had to line up with his teammates for a team photo. One year, instead of the photo being taken at the academy grounds, Bukayo and his teammates were treated to a surprise. They were going to line up on the field at the Emirates Stadium: the home of Arsenal FC.

Bukayo and his teammates were stunned into silence as they arrived at the stadium. They were guided to the field by the coaches and treated like professional players by the staff. After the team photo had been taken, the players were given a full tour.

Bukayo's eyes lit up as he arrived in the team changing room. The first-team players' shirts had been hung up and prepared for the upcoming game day. As the coach talked about the club's history, Bukayo wandered through the room. He noticed

the shirts of Mesut Özil and Alexis Sánchez. These were two of his favorite Arsenal players at the time. In less than a day, those players would be in this changing room and preparing for a match.

Bukayo's mind began to wonder and dream. The white letters on the back of the shirt shifted and moved. And as they settled back onto the Arsenal red, he saw a shirt that he hoped to wear in the future.

One that said: Saka.

★ ★ ★

As the years passed, Bukayo continued
to rise through the academy age
groups. But when he arrived at
the under 15s, he was met with an
astonishing surprise.

Bukayo discovered that his coach was
going to be none other than Freddie
Ljungberg, a famous left winger from
Arsenal's glory days. Ljungberg was
an Arsenal legend who had won
trophies, scored goals and had played
alongside some of the greatest players

to ever wear an Arsenal
shirt. Bukayo was going
to make sure he learned

as much as he possibly could from his new coach.

Ljungberg was impressed by Bukayo's determination and soon took him under his wing. He saw a bright spark in Bukayo and wanted to help him shine on the soccer field. Bukayo stayed under Ljungberg's coaching for a handful of years, all the way up until the U18s.

When Bukayo started playing for the U18s, Ljungberg put in a special recommendation to the coaches of the U23s setup. He believed that Bukayo had earned a shot at joining

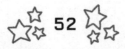

the team that was just one step below the first team. Bukayo had made his way through all of the age groups at Arsenal's Hale End Academy, and now he was getting his chance at London Colney—the training base for the Men's first team, the U23s and the Arsenal Ladies team. He had done so well to make it this far. How long would Bukayo have to wait to take that final step and become a senior team player for Arsenal?

7

EUROPEAN NIGHTS

Bukayo caught first-team coach Unai Emery's attention at London Colney. His effort, enthusiasm and leadership was clear.

Bukayo was given the opportunity to train with the first team by Emery. The Spaniard had been tasked with

moving Arsenal forward after the Arsene Wenger era, and Bukayo was a clear choice.

Arsenal were competing in the Europa League in the 2018/2019 season. During the group stage of the tournament, they had an away game against the Ukrainian side FC Vorskla Poltava. With Arsenal going undefeated in the first four games of the group stages, it gave the manager a chance to experiment with his lineup. Emery chose to rest many of his first-team players and look toward some of the rising stars in the U23s.

Bukayo and a handful of other players were selected as part of the squad for the match.

The players were flown over to Ukraine. Before Bukayo knew it, he was sitting on the bench for a professional soccer match. It wasn't exactly how he'd expected it—in Kyiv and on one of the coldest nights of his life—but he wouldn't have changed it for the world.

Bukayo was on the bench for the first half but promised game time in the second half. He wore a large coat with gloves as thick as oven mitts.

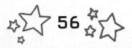

Arsenal blew away their opponents within forty-five minutes. Goals from Smith-Rowe, Aaron Ramsey and Joe Willock had provided a comfortable 0-3 lead.

In the second half, Bukayo was itching to get onto the field. He was excited to make his debut and have some match time, but also to get warmed up in the freezing cold. If he sat down any longer, he feared he'd lose his fingers or toes to frostbite!

In the 68th minute Emery answered Bukayo's prayer.

"Here we go, Bukayo. I'm bringing you on," said Emery.

"Thanks, boss!" said Bukayo, his teeth chattering.

Following a substitution, Bukayo sprinted onto the field to join his teammates. It was so cold that his breath misted in front of his face. In the twenty minutes that he was on the field, Bukayo did not stop running. While he usually played as a left winger, his versatility meant that he often played as a left back too. Emery put Bukayo in this defensive position to help keep a clean sheet

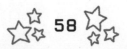

for his team. Bukayo gave it his all to achieve that target, and achieve it he did.

The referee brought his whistle to his mouth—Arsenal had got the win at 0-3. A part of Bukayo wanted to stay on the field and appreciate the moment in front of the traveling Arsenal fans. But in such freezing conditions, there was no chance he was going to do that. Instead, Bukayo ran for the warmth of the locker room.

While Bukayo had performed well on his debut, he was still not quite ready for first-team soccer in the

Premier League. But he was going to show the coaches that he'd be ready for the next time they needed him.

The final Europa League group stage match was only a couple of weeks later. Once more, Bukayo was selected for the squad. However, there was something special about this match that was missing from his first team debut. This was going to be Bukayo's first ever match at the Emirates Stadium. None of his friends and family had been able to travel to 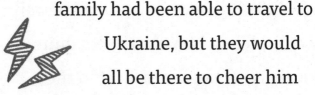 Ukraine, but they would all be there to cheer him on at the Arsenal home ground. He was finally going to achieve his dream of playing on that field.

After only getting a twenty-minute cameo against FC Vorskla Poltava, Bukayo was named in the starting lineup for the home tie against Qarabağ FK. This was a soccer team based in Azerbaijan. While the match wouldn't sell out an entire stadium and have full stands anxiously awaiting the kick off, it still meant alot to Bukayo.

Bukayo walked out of the tunnel with his Arsenal teammates, with the

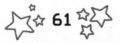

Europa League anthem blaring across the Emirates Stadium. As he stepped onto the field, he looked across the stadium knowing that his friends and family were somewhere in the stands supporting him. But despite his excitement, and his glowing pride at playing for Arsenal, Bukayo knew he couldn't be distracted. It was time to focus, and to prove to the manager that he deserved a place in this Arsenal squad.

In the 8th minute, Özil stole the ball in the opposition's half and fed it through to Bukayo. Bukayo cut inside

the defenders, noticed that space was available and tried to curl a shot in from range. The ball flew toward the goal, but it was met by gloves rather than the net. The Arsenal fans, who were holding their breath in anticipation, let out gasps and applauded the attempt. There was something special about this rising star, and the fans knew it.

In the 16th minute, Alexandre Lacazette wriggled his way through the Qarabağ FK box, which was

filled with defenders. On the right-hand side, at a tight angle, the Frenchman fired the ball across goal. The goalkeeper dived, but he could do nothing as the ball sailed past him and into the net. *Goal!* Bukayo celebrated with his teammates. They were 1-0 up in front of the home fans.

Neither side were able to change the scoreline before the first half ended. Having put in a strong performance, the manager decided to keep Bukayo on the field for the second half. Could Arsenal and Bukayo hold on for the win?

In the 65th minute, Ainsley Maitland-Niles sprinted down the right wing before sending a pass into the box. Bukayo ran on to it and shot. It was heading for the net, but a defender stuck out their leg and blocked it.

In the 76th minute, Bukayo had the ball on the left wing, he outskilled a defender and ran past him. He sent in a cross and his teammate Eddie Nketiah beat the defender to it. *Goal!* The fans cheered, and Bukayo ran to celebrate with Nketiah. But those celebrations did not last for long.

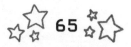

On the opposite side of the field, the linesman had his flag up. Nketiah was offside so the goal was ruled out.

In the 89th minute, Arsenal had a chance to wrap the match up. The Qarabağ FK players pushed forward in search of an equalizer. In doing so, they left holes in their defense. Maitland-Niles broke through for Arsenal and carried the ball forward. Bukayo joined him, sprinting as fast as he could, and found free space alone in the box. The ball was passed to him, and Bukayo swung his left foot at it. But once more, instead of finding the net, the ball cannoned off the goalkeeper and was cleared away. Bukayo stood there with his hands on his head. He had been so close to scoring his first senior goal!

The match stayed at 1-0. Arsenal had hung on, and Bukayo was a winner once more. Although he had not scored, he had been a constant menace to the opposition. Bukayo

walked around the field applauding the fans in each section of the stadium. His performance had given

the manager some thinking to do.
How far was Bukayo from being given
a chance in the Premier League?

8
ARTETA'S ARSENAL

On January 1st 2019, Bukayo was gifted his first ever Premier League start. Bukayo made a seven-minute appearance off the bench in a 4-1 win against Fulham. However, this was to be the last time the manager Emery played Bukayo in the league.

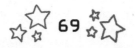

The Spanish manager was under huge pressure with his job. The club's board members believed that the more experienced players in the Arsenal squad would be able to turn the team's bad fortunes around. Because of this, Emery had to be careful about adding young players to his side. He tried his best to lead his team to Champions League qualification, but in the end he was unsuccessful. The board decided that it was time for a change, and Emery was removed as coach.

A familiar face arrived for a short stint in charge. Ljungberg, a

respected figure at the club, was given
an opportunity as the first team's
caretaker manager. He helped to
steady the ship, but after a month it
became clear that Arsenal needed
to bring in someone new to the side.
They needed a manager who would
engage the team and inspire a fan base
that was losing hope.

After careful consideration, the club
turned to Mikel Arteta.

Arteta had been learning how
to coach while working with Pep
Guardiola, Manchester City's manager
and one of the best coaches in the

world. Arteta was a former winger for Arsenal, and at one stage was the club's captain too. He understood what the club was like when it was firing on all cylinders. With his clever tactics and experience from his time with Guardiola, it appeared that Mikel Arteta was the man for the job.

Using players with experience instead of youth had not worked so well for Emery, so this was not the approach that Arteta planned to take. A key focus for him was to bring in talented players from the academy. This decision meant that Bukayo had the chance to play a lot more first-team soccer, but only if he proved that he was ready for it.

On the seventh matchday of the 2019/2020 Premier League campaign, Bukayo was named in the starting lineup for a match away at Manchester United. As Bukayo walked out onto the field and into the rain, he looked to the away fans. Only a few years ago, he had been sitting in those seats with his father watching Newcastle play. Now he was living his dream. He was playing for Arsenal as a professional soccer player in the Premier League.

Manchester United scored first thanks to a rocket of a shot from Scott McTominay. The midfielder fired the ball into the top left corner from outside of the box to send the home fans into hysteria. Not long after the half-time whistle blew, and Arteta needed to reset his players for the second half.

"I've liked a lot of what you've done out there," said Arteta. "We're at a disadvantage on their turf, and we've been putting up a good fight. We can get that goal back. We just need to make the most of our chances. Chase

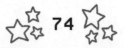

every last ball and I know we can get back into this game!"

The players returned to the field focussed and ready to attack. In the 58th minute, under pressure from Arsenal, Manchester United lost possession of the ball. Bukayo intercepted a loose pass and quickly played a through ball for his captain Aubameyang. The striker slotted the ball into the net, then the linesman put up his flag as he believed it to be offside. But there was still hope. VAR had recently been introduced in the league, and if there was any doubt

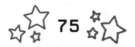

over goals scored or incidents, the system would be checked.

Following a VAR review, the referee was told the outcome. He brought his whistle to his mouth, signalled a square shape with his index fingers to reference the VAR and pointed to the halfway line. The goal had been given! The Arsenal players celebrated together, and Bukayo led the cheers with his goalscoring captain. Bukayo had just earned his first ever Premier League assist.

Following a hard-fought second half, both teams left the stadium with a point in a 1-1 draw. Bukayo had shown that he was more than just a young player breaking through. He was a talent that could make a real impact on this soccer team.

As such, Bukayo went on to earn twenty-six appearances in the league that season. He also went on to contribute five assists. But throughout the season, there was one thing that he simply couldn't achieve. He couldn't get that first Premier League goal. That was until the thirty-third matchday of the season, when Arsenal played away to Wolverhampton Wanderers.

Kieran Tierney found space and crossed the ball into the Wolves box. His intended target was Aubameyang, but a deflection off a defender caused the ball to fly into the air in the middle of the penalty box. Seeing an opportunity, Bukayo ran after the ball and met it on the volley with his left foot. The ball fired past Wolves" Rui Patrício. *Goal!* Bukayo had done it. He'd scored his first ever Premier League goal! Arsenal went on to win the match 0-2.

Arsenal finished eighth in the Premier League, and the campaign

was a disappointment overall. But the squad was beginning to gel together, and they appeared to be building momentum. Most importantly, the rising stars at the academy had made the most of their opportunity. Bukayo was no longer a developing player trying to break through, but a valued first-team player at Arsenal.

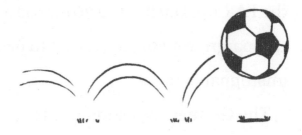

9
FIGHT FOR
THE FA CUP

Arsenal may not have had title
success in the Premier League,
but they performed superbly in
the FA Cup. During the 2019/2020
campaign, Arsenal appeared to be an
unstoppable force.

The Gunners defeated Leeds

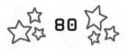

United in the third round to set up a fourth round encounter against Bournemouth. Bukayo played a crucial role in this tie, both scoring and assisting in a 2-1 win. With further wins against Portsmouth and Sheffield United, the team progressed to the cup semifinal. It was in this semifinal tie that most pundits expected Arsenal to crumble. This was because their opponents were the mighty Manchester City. Guardiola's side were flying high at the top of the Premier League and favorites to take the FA Cup trophy.

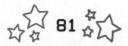

Against the odds, Arsenal prevailed with a 2-0 victory thanks to goals from Aubameyang. An exciting cup final was set for Wembley, against their London rivals Chelsea.

This matchup with Chelsea had an extra touch of drama. During Emery's term as manager, Arsenal had reached the Europa League final. Their opponents on that night were none other than Chelsea. It was the blues who were victorious on that night in Baku and Arsenal.

Now Arsenal were out for revenge. This time, they were going to make sure they were victorious.

To the surprise of many, Bukayo was left on the bench for the final. He had been a standout player for the side during the season, and this left many spectators scratching their heads over the decision.

However, it was important to remember that soccer is a team sport, and a manager has an entire squad to use. Bukayo had played a lot of league soccer in the cup and the manager saw it as an opportunity to rest him and

rotate his squad. While Bukayo would have loved to be on the field, he was still happy to support his teammates from the bench.

The players emerged from the tunnel to a silent stadium. No fans were allowed to attend the final due to COVID-19 restrictions. But that didn't stop the millions of fans from watching at home and cheering on their teams.

It was Chelsea that struck first. In the 5th minute, Christian Pulisic latched onto a loose ball in the box and dinked it over Emiliano Martínez, the Arsenal goalkeeper. The Chelsea players cheered in delight. As the Arsenal players walked back into position, Bukayo rose from his seat and cupped his hands to his mouth.

"It's still early!" said Bukayo. "Come on, heads up. We've got this!"

Aubameyang heard Bukayo's shout and nodded to him.

In the 26th minute, Aubameyang was sent a through ball and sprinted toward the Chelsea box. Chelsea's captain, César Azpilicueta, tried to chase him. Knowing that Aubameyang was far faster than him, Azpilicueta's

only option was to grab his shoulder and try to slow him down. But he applied too much force and fouled Aubameyang. The referee pointed to the spot. It was a penalty.

Aubameyang placed the ball on the penalty spot and ran to kick it. Bukayo was on his feet with the rest of the benched players, watching every step and hoping for the equalizer. Aubameyang struck the ball forcefully to the right. The Chelsea goalkeeper dived to the left. *Goal!* Bukayo and the other substitutes leapt into the air and celebrated. They were back level, and

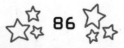

still in with a chance of winning the FA Cup.

The two teams went back and forth in waves of attack, without either being able to find a second goal to take the lead. But in the 67th minute, a charging break by Héctor Bellerín broke through the Chelsea midfield. Bellerín was tackled, but his teammate Nicholas Pépé was the first to get to the loose ball. The winger tucked inside and found Aubameyang. The

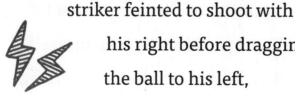

striker feinted to shoot with his right before dragging the ball to his left,

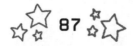

sweeping past the last defender. From

a tight angle, Aubameyang

chipped the ball up and

over the goalkeeper.

Goal! Arsenal were

in the lead with only

twenty or so minutes still

to play. Could they hang on?

In an attempt to improve their

chances of holding the lead, Arteta

made a number of defensive

substitutions. Bukayo was

disappointed, as that meant that he

would not get onto the field himself.

But that did not stop him supporting

his team to the final minute. After a lengthy injury time at the end of the match, the referee finally brought the whistle to his mouth. Arsenal had done it!

Bukayo's team were FA Cup champions. The rising star may not have played in the final, but he had played an enormous role in the cup matches leading up to it. Without his contributions, the side would not have even made it to the final, let alone won it.

Bukayo was presented with a winner's medal, along with the rest

of the Arsenal squad, to reward their victory. After they received their medals, it was time for the part every fan and player looks forward to the most. As captain, Aubameyang picked up the FA Cup trophy from its perch and paraded it in front of his teammates. The squad all held out their hands and stamped their feet in anticipation. Their captain lifted the trophy above his head and let out a passionate cheer. Bukayo and his teammates cheered as loud as they could. It didn't matter if they lost their voices, this was a moment that they

were going to cherish forever. During the 2019/2020 season, Arsenal were the FA Cup champions!

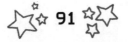

10
THE THREE LIONS

Bukayo's breakthrough season for Arsenal had people in the wider soccer community talking. He had quickly become one of the most highly rated youngsters in English soccer, and as such rumors were spreading that he was being

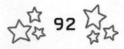

considered for a spot in the England squad. The national side had set up a friendly against Wales, alongside two Nations League games against Belgium and Denmark. It turned out that the rumors about Bukayo were true. England manager Gareth Southgate selected him in his squad of thirty players for the upcoming fixtures.

Bukayo had played for England in their academy setup, so a trip to St. George's Park was nothing new to him. However, the fieldes would be. He was used to playing on the

back fieldes with the England junior players, but this time he was going to be training with the first-team squad on the main fieldes. As a teenager he'd looked over at them longingly, trying to catch a glimpse of the professionals. Now, he was there as a pro himself—someone who the junior players wanted to see.

Bukayo was dropped off at St. George's Park and met by a small crowd. He was one of the most talked about players, so photographers were keen to get as many snaps of him as they could.

Bukayo was not the only player to be receiving their first senior call-up for England. Dominic Calvert-Lewin, Harvey Barnes and Reece James were also joining the camp. It also helped that Arsenal's Maitland-Niles was a part of the England squad at the time, so Bukayo had a familiar face that he could rely on in the camp.

Bukayo took to training well. He impressed the national side's coaches, just as he had at every level before.

His versatility as a player would be a valuable asset to a talented squad. While he was usually a left-sided winger for Arsenal, he had played as a left back previously and could switch flanks too. Being a player with such flexibility put him in good stead on the international stage, where many talented players compete for selection in the final squad, let alone the glory of being named in the starting lineup.

Because of Bukayo's hard work, he was rewarded with a spot in the

starting lineup for the friendly against Wales. With two important competitive fixtures coming up after the friendly, Southgate chose to rest some of the key players and give the younger team members a chance to shine at Wembley. Once again, COVID-19 prevented fans from attending, so Bukayo didn't have his friends and family in the stadium to cheer him on. But that wouldn't stop him.

In the 25th minute, Jack Grealish dazzled the Welsh defenders and crossed the ball into the box. Bukayo and Calvert-Lewin raced into the

penalty area. Bukayo's run drew out the defenders while the tall Calvert-Lewin leapt into the air and met the ball with his head. It flew past the goalkeeper and hit the net. *Goal!* England were leading 1-0.

In the 53rd minute, Connor Coady, one of England's center-backs, scored the second goal. Kieran Tripper swung in a dangerous curling cross that Coady ran onto and poked into the goal. Bukayo was a youngster just

 coming into the England setup while Coady was a player who had much

more experience, but only on the domestic stage. Even so, his hard work with Wolverhampton Wanderers had earned him some playing time with England. As he scored, the defender's shout of delight could be heard across the empty stadium. With a beaming smile, Bukayo went over to congratulate him on one of the proudest moments of Coady's soccer career.

A Danny Ings overhead kick cemented the win for England, and Bukayo finished his debut performance with a 3-0 victory.

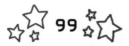

Playing for England was an honor. And now that Bukayo knew just how amazing it felt, he wanted to be in this team for years to come.

11
A SHINING
LIGHT

Arteta had been given a fresh start at Arsenal. Even with the team finishing the 2019/2020 season in a disappointing eighth place, he had been given the freedom to find space for the younger squad members within his starting eleven. He was also

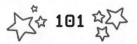

free to develop a new style of playing at the club.

Despite Arsenal's poor Premier League finish, by winning the FA Cup Arteta had brought great pride to a club that had appeared to be on a downward spiral. But could Arsenal improve their league standing in the 2020/2021 campaign?

During the summer transfer window, the club signed Willian, Gabriel and Thomas Partey in the hope that these experienced players would help bring firepower to the club's weaponry. But as the season went on, these hopes and dreams failed to produce results. The new experienced players took time to settle in at the club.

Inconsistent performances from the side as a whole led to another eighth place finish in the Premier League. Unlike the previous season in their 2020/2021 campaign, Arsenal found no success in a domestic cup either. There was nowhere for the management to hide.

Despite this disappointment there was a small feeling of hope, because this was the year of Bukayo Saka.

Throughout the campaign, Bukayo wowed fans. He had improved even more from the year before, and at such a young age he had already become a first-team star. He made thirty-two appearances in the league and provided four assists plus five goals. He was one of the first names on the team sheet for almost every encounter, and a player who Arteta could rely on to put in a determined performance.

Bukayo's goals helped his side earn important points during wins against Sheffield United, Chelsea, West Bromwich, Newcastle and

Southampton. It was clear for all to see that this young star was the player Arsenal should build their team around. The club had unearthed a soccer talent that was not only going to wow fans at Arsenal, but surely had a long career ahead of him with England too.

As a result of Bukayo's performances, he was nominated for the Player of the Year award at Arsenal's end-of-year ceremony.

 Bukayo had been dreaming of making his debut for the club, never mind

taking part in the majority of league matches and being nominated for such an award.

The award is given based on the votes of Arsenal supporters, and to receive it is a great honor for any player. The votes had been counted and the 2020/2021 winner was Bukayo Saka!

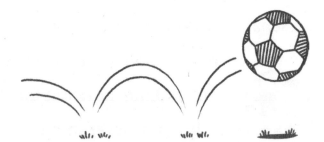

12

EURO 2020

Bukayo's strong performances
for Arsenal earned him a spot in
England's squad for the European
Championships. To be named
in a squad for an international
tournament was impressive in itself.
But to be named in one at only 19 was
astonishing. Bukayo was a serious

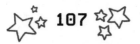

talent, and a star that shone so brightly he could not be ignored by the England manager.

Bukayo's playfulness and constant smile did him no harm in the England training camp. His easy going nature allowed him to bond quickly with his teammates, and add to the feeling of unity and hope in the squad. Bukayo enjoyed playing pranks on his teammates, and

 whenever a camera was filming him, he would often play up to it and make everyone laugh.

Each and every player truly believed that this was going to be the year for England, and Bukayo was determined to play his part, no matter what role that would end up being. No matter what happened in this tournament, Bukayo was going to make sure that he had given it his all.

Before the tournament began, each member of the squad was gifted a new suit. The whole squad were to put them on and come together for a team photo. Bukayo went off to the changing rooms and unzipped his suit from its bag. It was a smart blue suit

and tie, tailor-made just for him. Beaming from ear-to-ear, Bukayo changed into the suit, looked himself over in the mirrors and walked through a hall where a couple of his teammates were sitting and chatting.

"Hey, Bukayo!" Jordan Henderson called. "Come over here."

"Looking sharp, bud!" said Bukayo as he walked over to Henderson, an established midfielder and captain of the Liverpool side.

"You're not long out of school, but you seem to have forgotten your tie-

knotting skills!" Henderson laughed.

Bukayo grinned and looked down at the tie around his neck. "What's wrong with it?"

"Here, let me just tighten it up a bit," said Henderson.

Despite playing for rival clubs across the Premier League, all of the England players united to form one close-knit group. Putting their rivalries aside led to a clear and united goal of helping England succeed in the Euros.

England had been drawn in a group with Croatia, Scotland and Czech Republic. If the team had hopes of

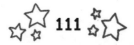

going further in the competition, they
had to avoid getting knocked out of
the group.

The team started off on the right
foot with a 1-0 victory against Croatia,
but were then held to a 0-0 draw
against Scotland. Bukayo did not
play in either of these games. But he
refused to give up hope of playing.
He trained as hard as he could
between matches, and Southgate
saw his hunger. As a result, for the
final group stage match against the
Czech Republic, Bukayo was selected
in the starting lineup. In front of a

reduced-capacity crowd at Wembley Stadium, Bukayo was making his first international tournament appearance for England.

In the 12th minute, Bukayo received the ball in his own half and burst forward. He ran past a handful of defenders before passing to Kalvin Phillips. The midfielder returned the ball to Bukayo who crossed the

ball into the box. But no one was able to reach it. Grealish picked up the cross on the opposite side of the

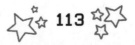

field and fired it into the box again. Raheem Sterling rose above the defenders and nodded the ball into the back of the net. *Goal!* England were leading 1-0, and Bukayo had played a crucial role in an England goal.

England managed to hold on to the lead and took the three points for the win. With this, they ensured their progression from the group as winners to set up a tie against

Germany. Bukayo's performance in that match had wowed anyone who had

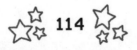

watched it. Pundits and fans alike believed that Bukayo could not be dropped from the team. He was voted Man of the Match, and his performance had fans dreaming of going far in the tournament.

And go far they did. England then defeated Germany, Ukraine and Denmark in the knockout stages. Bukayo provided a pivotal assist during England's comeback win against Denmark. England made it all the way to the final of the tournament. In front of a packed-out Wembley Stadium, England

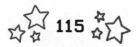

were playing Italy for the right to be crowned as winners of Euro 2020.

Luke Shaw got England off to the perfect start in the final, with the left back scoring in the 2nd minute to send the fans in the stadium, and millions of fans watching at home, into delirious celebration.

But the tide turned in the second half. In the 67th minute, Italy's Leonardo Bonucci, equalized bringing the teams level once more. Neither side could find a winner during the ninety minutes, nor could they find one in extra time. Just as it

had been for England in many past
tournaments, penalties would be
needed to decide a winner.

Brave players from both sides
stepped up to take their penalty kicks.
England's Harry Kane and Harry
Maguire scored their kicks, as did
Italy's Domenico Berardi, Bonucci
and Federico Bernardeschi. England's
Marcus Rashford hit the post, while
Jadon Sancho saw his effort saved by
the towering Gianluigi Donnarumma.

England's goalkeeper, Jordan
Pickford, kept the match alive by
denying Andrea Belotti and Jorginho,

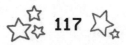

but to stay in the match England needed to score their fifth penalty. Bukayo, with his heart racing, had nominated himself for a penalty. The thousands of fans in attendance watched on as Bukayo slowly walked up to the penalty spot. He placed the ball down carefully, taking a breath to calm his nerves. The whistle blew and he ran toward the ball. Bukayo had enjoyed one of the best summers of his life, but with one kick that

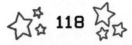

night turned into one of the worst.

Bukayo shot to the right. Donnarumma met the ball with strong hands and pushed it away. Italy had won Euro 2020. Bukayo stood still with his head in his hands. His heart sunk and tears came like a flood. How could it end this way?

Southgate walked over to Bukayo and hugged him.

"I know it hurts, but this isn't on you," he said to Bukayo. "You're a star. This is not the moment that defines you."

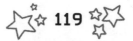

One by one Bukayo's England
teammates surrounded him and
huddled. On that field, England ended
the tournament as they had started it:
as a brotherhood. As a team.

13

ROAD TO QATAR 2022

Despite the heartbreaking end to the Euro 2020 campaign, the England team had made their country proud. They had made it all the way to the final of an international tournament for the first time since 1966. They had inspired a generation of young soccer

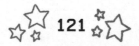

players to be as strong and determined as they had been.

When Bukayo returned to pre-season training with Arsenal, he was greeted by a wall of messages from supporters. A minority of supporters criticized the players for losing and aimed vile racist remarks at Bukayo. However, the overwhelming majority of fans across the country were proud of him and wanted to show that there was no place for hate or racism in

soccer. To demonstrate this, thousands of fans sent in messages to show their

admiration for Bukayo's bravery and efforts.

Bukayo made his way across the training field and over to a wall where the messages were displayed. Not a brick could be seen—only thousands of pieces of paper all with messages for him. Bukayo slowly walked along the wall, left speechless by the messages as he made an effort to read every last one. The messages had come from children and adults alike. All of them wanted to show their appreciation for his hard work during the tournament. One kind fan had even sent in his

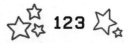

pocket money for Bukayo, and another had promised that if they played soccer in the park together, he'd let Bukayo win!

Bukayo was overwhelmed by all of the heartfelt messages. With the help of some club staff, all of them were placed into boxes for him to take home.

During the summer of 2021, Arsenal took part in a series of local friendlies

in the capital to show support for environmentally-friendly soccer. This meant that Arsenal were playing a friendly against their not-so-friendly rivals Tottenham Hotspur.

The two teams had fought against each other for decades to be the pride of North London. But when Bukayo was brought on as a substitute in the game, every fan in the stadium put aside their rivalry. Each individual, whether they were in red or white, stood up to applaud him. Surprised by this gesture, Bukayo applauded all of the fans in the stadium.

After the dust had settled on Euro 2020, Bukayo's family all came together to surprise him, and to

celebrate his achievements. In such
a busy and exciting summer, it was
easy to forget that Bukayo was still
only 19 years old.

He'd come so far from those days
kicking a ball about at Perivale
Park. He'd come so far from sitting
in classrooms with his Arsenal
teammates. He'd not only broken
into the Arsenal first team, but
he was one of the club's
star players. He'd not
only broken into
the England squad,
but he had done

enough to play in the final of a major international tournament. And all of these achievements had come at such a young age.

★ ★ ★

Bukayo has an incredible soccer career ahead of him. Will he be an Arsenal legend playing for the club for years to come? Will he be the superstar that finally brings home a World Cup or European Championship for England?

Those questions are yet to be

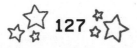

answered. However, there is one thing that's certain: Bukayo Saka is a rising star, and a player whose light shines incredibly brightly.